This Book Belongs To

DATE: _____

Counting your Blessings

Each day offers many blessings. We can easily miss them in our daily toils.
Appreciate them here, no matter how small they may seem.

_____

_____

_____

_____

People that Matter

The people in our life plays a tremendous role in our personal happiness. Recognize them here and
how they made your day brighter. Don't focus on the negative energy given off by some.

_____

_____

_____

_____

How I Matter

Our purpose here is to enrich the lives of those we care about. What did you do or could have
done to be a blessing for others today?

_____

_____

_____

_____

DATE: _____

Counting your Blessings

Each day offers many blessings. We can easily miss them in our daily toils.
Appreciate them here, no matter how small they may seem.

_____
_____
_____
_____

People that Matter

The people in our life plays a tremendous role in our personal happiness. Recognize them here and
how they made your day brighter. Don't focus on the negative energy given off by some.

_____
_____
_____
_____

How I Matter

Our purpose here is to enrich the lives of those we care about. What did you do or could have
done to be a blessing for others today?

_____
_____
_____
_____

DATE: _____

Counting your Blessings

Each day offers many blessings. We can easily miss them in our daily toils.
Appreciate them here, no matter how small they may seem.

_____

_____

_____

_____

People that Matter

The people in our life plays a tremendous role in our personal happiness. Recognize them here and
how they made your day brighter. Don't focus on the negative energy given off by some.

_____

_____

_____

_____

How I Matter

Our purpose here is to enrich the lives of those we care about. What did you do or could have
done to be a blessing for others today?

_____

_____

_____

_____

DATE: _____

Counting your Blessings

Each day offers many blessings. We can easily miss them in our daily toils.
Appreciate them here, no matter how small they may seem.

_____

_____

_____

_____

People that Matter

The people in our life plays a tremendous role in our personal happiness. Recognize them here and
how they made your day brighter. Don't focus on the negative energy given off by some.

_____

_____

_____

_____

How I Matter

Our purpose here is to enrich the lives of those we care about. What did you do or could have
done to be a blessing for others today?

_____

_____

_____

_____

DATE: _____

Counting your Blessings

Each day offers many blessings. We can easily miss them in our daily toils.
Appreciate them here, no matter how small they may seem.

_____

_____

_____

_____

People that Matter

The people in our life plays a tremendous role in our personal happiness. Recognize them here and
how they made your day brighter. Don't focus on the negative energy given off by some.

_____

_____

_____

_____

How I Matter

Our purpose here is to enrich the lives of those we care about. What did you do or could have
done to be a blessing for others today?

_____

_____

_____

_____

DATE: _____

Counting your Blessings

Each day offers many blessings. We can easily miss them in our daily toils.
Appreciate them here, no matter how small they may seem.

_____

_____

_____

_____

People that Matter

The people in our life plays a tremendous role in our personal happiness. Recognize them here and
how they made your day brighter. Don't focus on the negative energy given off by some.

_____

_____

_____

_____

How I Matter

Our purpose here is to enrich the lives of those we care about. What did you do or could have
done to be a blessing for others today?

_____

_____

_____

_____

DATE: _____

Counting your Blessings

Each day offers many blessings. We can easily miss them in our daily toils.
Appreciate them here, no matter how small they may seem.

_____

_____

_____

_____

People that Matter

The people in our life plays a tremendous role in our personal happiness. Recognize them here and
how they made your day brighter. Don't focus on the negative energy given off by some.

_____

_____

_____

_____

How I Matter

Our purpose here is to enrich the lives of those we care about. What did you do or could have
done to be a blessing for others today?

_____

_____

_____

_____

DATE: _____

Counting your Blessings

Each day offers many blessings. We can easily miss them in our daily toils.
Appreciate them here, no matter how small they may seem.

_____

_____

_____

People that Matter

The people in our life plays a tremendous role in our personal happiness. Recognize them here and
how they made your day brighter. Don't focus on the negative energy given off by some.

_____

_____

_____

How I Matter

Our purpose here is to enrich the lives of those we care about. What did you do or could have
done to be a blessing for others today?

_____

_____

_____

DATE: _____

Counting your Blessings

Each day offers many blessings. We can easily miss them in our daily toils.
Appreciate them here, no matter how small they may seem.

_____

_____

_____

_____

People that Matter

The people in our life plays a tremendous role in our personal happiness. Recognize them here and
how they made your day brighter. Don't focus on the negative energy given off by some.

_____

_____

_____

_____

How I Matter

Our purpose here is to enrich the lives of those we care about. What did you do or could have
done to be a blessing for others today?

_____

_____

_____

_____

DATE: _____

Counting your Blessings

Each day offers many blessings. We can easily miss them in our daily toils.
Appreciate them here, no matter how small they may seem.

_____

_____

_____

_____

People that Matter

The people in our life plays a tremendous role in our personal happiness. Recognize them here and
how they made your day brighter. Don't focus on the negative energy given off by some.

_____

_____

_____

_____

How I Matter

Our purpose here is to enrich the lives of those we care about. What did you do or could have
done to be a blessing for others today?

_____

_____

_____

_____

DATE: _____

Counting your Blessings

Each day offers many blessings. We can easily miss them in our daily toils.
Appreciate them here, no matter how small they may seem.

_____
_____
_____
_____

People that Matter

The people in our life plays a tremendous role in our personal happiness. Recognize them here and
how they made your day brighter. Don't focus on the negative energy given off by some.

_____
_____
_____
_____

How I Matter

Our purpose here is to enrich the lives of those we care about. What did you do or could have
done to be a blessing for others today?

_____
_____
_____
_____

DATE: _____

Counting your Blessings

Each day offers many blessings. We can easily miss them in our daily toils.
Appreciate them here, no matter how small they may seem.

_____

_____

_____

People that Matter

The people in our life plays a tremendous role in our personal happiness. Recognize them here and
how they made your day brighter. Don't focus on the negative energy given off by some.

_____

_____

_____

How I Matter

Our purpose here is to enrich the lives of those we care about. What did you do or could have
done to be a blessing for others today?

_____

_____

_____

DATE: _____

Counting your Blessings

Each day offers many blessings. We can easily miss them in our daily toils. Appreciate them here, no matter how small they may seem.

_____

_____

_____

_____

People that Matter

The people in our life plays a tremendous role in our personal happiness. Recognize them here and how they made your day brighter. Don't focus on the negative energy given off by some.

_____

_____

_____

_____

How I Matter

Our purpose here is to enrich the lives of those we care about. What did you do or could have done to be a blessing for others today?

_____

_____

_____

_____

DATE: _____

Counting your Blessings

Each day offers many blessings. We can easily miss them in our daily toils.
Appreciate them here, no matter how small they may seem.

_____

_____

_____

People that Matter

The people in our life plays a tremendous role in our personal happiness. Recognize them here and
how they made your day brighter. Don't focus on the negative energy given off by some.

_____

_____

_____

How I Matter

Our purpose here is to enrich the lives of those we care about. What did you do or could have
done to be a blessing for others today?

_____

_____

_____

DATE: _____

Counting your Blessings

Each day offers many blessings. We can easily miss them in our daily toils.
Appreciate them here, no matter how small they may seem.

_____

_____

_____

_____

People that Matter

The people in our life plays a tremendous role in our personal happiness. Recognize them here and
how they made your day brighter. Don't focus on the negative energy given off by some.

_____

_____

_____

_____

How I Matter

Our purpose here is to enrich the lives of those we care about. What did you do or could have
done to be a blessing for others today?

_____

_____

_____

_____

DATE: _____

Counting your Blessings

Each day offers many blessings. We can easily miss them in our daily toils.
Appreciate them here, no matter how small they may seem.

_____

_____

_____

_____

People that Matter

The people in our life plays a tremendous role in our personal happiness. Recognize them here and
how they made your day brighter. Don't focus on the negative energy given off by some.

_____

_____

_____

_____

How I Matter

Our purpose here is to enrich the lives of those we care about. What did you do or could have
done to be a blessing for others today?

_____

_____

_____

_____

DATE: _____

Counting your Blessings

Each day offers many blessings. We can easily miss them in our daily toils.
Appreciate them here, no matter how small they may seem.

_____

_____

_____

People that Matter

The people in our life plays a tremendous role in our personal happiness. Recognize them here and
how they made your day brighter. Don't focus on the negative energy given off by some.

_____

_____

_____

How I Matter

Our purpose here is to enrich the lives of those we care about. What did you do or could have
done to be a blessing for others today?

_____

_____

_____

_____

DATE: _____

Counting your Blessings

Each day offers many blessings. We can easily miss them in our daily toils.
Appreciate them here, no matter how small they may seem.

_____
_____
_____
_____

People that Matter

The people in our life plays a tremendous role in our personal happiness. Recognize them here and
how they made your day brighter. Don't focus on the negative energy given off by some.

_____
_____
_____
_____

How I Matter

Our purpose here is to enrich the lives of those we care about. What did you do or could have
done to be a blessing for others today?

_____
_____
_____
_____

DATE: _____

Counting your Blessings

Each day offers many blessings. We can easily miss them in our daily toils.
Appreciate them here, no matter how small they may seem.

_____

_____

_____

_____

People that Matter

The people in our life plays a tremendous role in our personal happiness. Recognize them here and
how they made your day brighter. Don't focus on the negative energy given off by some.

_____

_____

_____

_____

How I Matter

Our purpose here is to enrich the lives of those we care about. What did you do or could have
done to be a blessing for others today?

_____

_____

_____

_____

DATE: _____

Counting your Blessings

Each day offers many blessings. We can easily miss them in our daily toils.
Appreciate them here, no matter how small they may seem.

_____

_____

_____

People that Matter

The people in our life plays a tremendous role in our personal happiness. Recognize them here and
how they made your day brighter. Don't focus on the negative energy given off by some.

_____

_____

_____

How I Matter

Our purpose here is to enrich the lives of those we care about. What did you do or could have
done to be a blessing for others today?

_____

_____

_____

_____

DATE: _____

Counting your Blessings

Each day offers many blessings. We can easily miss them in our daily toils.
Appreciate them here, no matter how small they may seem.

_____

_____

_____

_____

People that Matter

The people in our life plays a tremendous role in our personal happiness. Recognize them here and
how they made your day brighter. Don't focus on the negative energy given off by some.

_____

_____

_____

_____

How I Matter

Our purpose here is to enrich the lives of those we care about. What did you do or could have
done to be a blessing for others today?

_____

_____

_____

_____

DATE: _____

Counting your Blessings

Each day offers many blessings. We can easily miss them in our daily toils.
Appreciate them here, no matter how small they may seem.

_____

_____

_____

_____

People that Matter

The people in our life plays a tremendous role in our personal happiness. Recognize them here and
how they made your day brighter. Don't focus on the negative energy given off by some.

_____

_____

_____

_____

How I Matter

Our purpose here is to enrich the lives of those we care about. What did you do or could have
done to be a blessing for others today?

_____

_____

_____

_____

DATE: _____

Counting your Blessings

Each day offers many blessings. We can easily miss them in our daily toils.
Appreciate them here, no matter how small they may seem.

_____

_____

_____

_____

People that Matter

The people in our life plays a tremendous role in our personal happiness. Recognize them here and
how they made your day brighter. Don't focus on the negative energy given off by some.

_____

_____

_____

_____

How I Matter

Our purpose here is to enrich the lives of those we care about. What did you do or could have
done to be a blessing for others today?

_____

_____

_____

_____

DATE: _____

Counting your Blessings

Each day offers many blessings. We can easily miss them in our daily toils.
Appreciate them here, no matter how small they may seem.

_____
_____
_____
_____

People that Matter

The people in our life plays a tremendous role in our personal happiness. Recognize them here and
how they made your day brighter. Don't focus on the negative energy given off by some.

_____
_____
_____
_____

How I Matter

Our purpose here is to enrich the lives of those we care about. What did you do or could have
done to be a blessing for others today?

_____
_____
_____
_____

DATE: _____

Counting your Blessings

Each day offers many blessings. We can easily miss them in our daily toils.
Appreciate them here, no matter how small they may seem.

_____
_____
_____
_____

People that Matter

The people in our life plays a tremendous role in our personal happiness. Recognize them here and
how they made your day brighter. Don't focus on the negative energy given off by some.

_____
_____
_____
_____

How I Matter

Our purpose here is to enrich the lives of those we care about. What did you do or could have
done to be a blessing for others today?

_____
_____
_____
_____

DATE: _____

Counting your Blessings

Each day offers many blessings. We can easily miss them in our daily toils.
Appreciate them here, no matter how small they may seem.

_____

_____

_____

_____

People that Matter

The people in our life plays a tremendous role in our personal happiness. Recognize them here and
how they made your day brighter. Don't focus on the negative energy given off by some.

_____

_____

_____

_____

How I Matter

Our purpose here is to enrich the lives of those we care about. What did you do or could have
done to be a blessing for others today?

_____

_____

_____

_____

DATE: _____

Counting your Blessings

Each day offers many blessings. We can easily miss them in our daily toils.
Appreciate them here, no matter how small they may seem.

_____

_____

_____

People that Matter

The people in our life plays a tremendous role in our personal happiness. Recognize them here and
how they made your day brighter. Don't focus on the negative energy given off by some.

_____

_____

_____

How I Matter

Our purpose here is to enrich the lives of those we care about. What did you do or could have
done to be a blessing for others today?

_____

_____

_____

DATE: _____

Counting your Blessings

Each day offers many blessings. We can easily miss them in our daily toils.
Appreciate them here, no matter how small they may seem.

_____

_____

_____

People that Matter

The people in our life plays a tremendous role in our personal happiness. Recognize them here and
how they made your day brighter. Don't focus on the negative energy given off by some.

_____

_____

_____

How I Matter

Our purpose here is to enrich the lives of those we care about. What did you do or could have
done to be a blessing for others today?

_____

_____

_____

DATE: _____

Counting your Blessings

Each day offers many blessings. We can easily miss them in our daily toils.
Appreciate them here, no matter how small they may seem.

_____

_____

_____

_____

People that Matter

The people in our life plays a tremendous role in our personal happiness. Recognize them here and
how they made your day brighter. Don't focus on the negative energy given off by some.

_____

_____

_____

_____

How I Matter

Our purpose here is to enrich the lives of those we care about. What did you do or could have
done to be a blessing for others today?

_____

_____

_____

_____

DATE: _____

Counting your Blessings

Each day offers many blessings. We can easily miss them in our daily toils.
Appreciate them here, no matter how small they may seem.

_____

_____

_____

_____

People that Matter

The people in our life plays a tremendous role in our personal happiness. Recognize them here and
how they made your day brighter. Don't focus on the negative energy given off by some.

_____

_____

_____

_____

How I Matter

Our purpose here is to enrich the lives of those we care about. What did you do or could have
done to be a blessing for others today?

_____

_____

_____

_____

DATE: _____

Counting your Blessings

Each day offers many blessings. We can easily miss them in our daily toils.
Appreciate them here, no matter how small they may seem.

_____

_____

_____

_____

People that Matter

The people in our life plays a tremendous role in our personal happiness. Recognize them here and
how they made your day brighter. Don't focus on the negative energy given off by some.

_____

_____

_____

_____

How I Matter

Our purpose here is to enrich the lives of those we care about. What did you do or could have
done to be a blessing for others today?

_____

_____

_____

_____

DATE: _____

Counting your Blessings

Each day offers many blessings. We can easily miss them in our daily toils.
Appreciate them here, no matter how small they may seem.

_____

_____

_____

_____

People that Matter

The people in our life plays a tremendous role in our personal happiness. Recognize them here and
how they made your day brighter. Don't focus on the negative energy given off by some.

_____

_____

_____

_____

How I Matter

Our purpose here is to enrich the lives of those we care about. What did you do or could have
done to be a blessing for others today?

_____

_____

_____

_____

DATE: _____

Counting your Blessings

Each day offers many blessings. We can easily miss them in our daily toils.
Appreciate them here, no matter how small they may seem.

_____

_____

_____

_____

People that Matter

The people in our life plays a tremendous role in our personal happiness. Recognize them here and
how they made your day brighter. Don't focus on the negative energy given off by some.

_____

_____

_____

_____

How I Matter

Our purpose here is to enrich the lives of those we care about. What did you do or could have
done to be a blessing for others today?

_____

_____

_____

_____

DATE: _____

Counting your Blessings

Each day offers many blessings. We can easily miss them in our daily toils.
Appreciate them here, no matter how small they may seem.

_____

_____

_____

_____

People that Matter

The people in our life plays a tremendous role in our personal happiness. Recognize them here and
how they made your day brighter. Don't focus on the negative energy given off by some.

_____

_____

_____

_____

How I Matter

Our purpose here is to enrich the lives of those we care about. What did you do or could have
done to be a blessing for others today?

_____

_____

_____

_____

DATE: _____

Counting your Blessings

Each day offers many blessings. We can easily miss them in our daily toils.
Appreciate them here, no matter how small they may seem.

_____

_____

_____

_____

People that Matter

The people in our life plays a tremendous role in our personal happiness. Recognize them here and
how they made your day brighter. Don't focus on the negative energy given off by some.

_____

_____

_____

_____

How I Matter

Our purpose here is to enrich the lives of those we care about. What did you do or could have
done to be a blessing for others today?

_____

_____

_____

_____

DATE: _____

Counting your Blessings

Each day offers many blessings. We can easily miss them in our daily toils.
Appreciate them here, no matter how small they may seem.

_____

_____

_____

_____

People that Matter

The people in our life plays a tremendous role in our personal happiness. Recognize them here and
how they made your day brighter. Don't focus on the negative energy given off by some.

_____

_____

_____

_____

How I Matter

Our purpose here is to enrich the lives of those we care about. What did you do or could have
done to be a blessing for others today?

_____

_____

_____

_____

DATE: _____

Counting your Blessings

Each day offers many blessings. We can easily miss them in our daily toils.
Appreciate them here, no matter how small they may seem.

_____

_____

_____

_____

People that Matter

The people in our life plays a tremendous role in our personal happiness. Recognize them here and
how they made your day brighter. Don't focus on the negative energy given off by some.

_____

_____

_____

_____

How I Matter

Our purpose here is to enrich the lives of those we care about. What did you do or could have
done to be a blessing for others today?

_____

_____

_____

_____

DATE: _____

Counting your Blessings

Each day offers many blessings. We can easily miss them in our daily toils.
Appreciate them here, no matter how small they may seem.

_____
_____
_____
_____

People that Matter

The people in our life plays a tremendous role in our personal happiness. Recognize them here and
how they made your day brighter. Don't focus on the negative energy given off by some.

_____
_____
_____
_____

How I Matter

Our purpose here is to enrich the lives of those we care about. What did you do or could have
done to be a blessing for others today?

_____
_____
_____
_____

DATE: _____

Counting your Blessings

Each day offers many blessings. We can easily miss them in our daily toils.
Appreciate them here, no matter how small they may seem.

_____

_____

_____

People that Matter

The people in our life plays a tremendous role in our personal happiness. Recognize them here and
how they made your day brighter. Don't focus on the negative energy given off by some.

_____

_____

_____

How I Matter

Our purpose here is to enrich the lives of those we care about. What did you do or could have
done to be a blessing for others today?

_____

_____

_____

_____

DATE: _____

Counting your Blessings

Each day offers many blessings. We can easily miss them in our daily toils.
Appreciate them here, no matter how small they may seem.

_____

_____

_____

People that Matter

The people in our life plays a tremendous role in our personal happiness. Recognize them here and
how they made your day brighter. Don't focus on the negative energy given off by some.

_____

_____

_____

How I Matter

Our purpose here is to enrich the lives of those we care about. What did you do or could have
done to be a blessing for others today?

_____

_____

_____

_____

DATE: _____

Counting your Blessings

Each day offers many blessings. We can easily miss them in our daily toils.
Appreciate them here, no matter how small they may seem.

_____

_____

_____

_____

People that Matter

The people in our life plays a tremendous role in our personal happiness. Recognize them here and
how they made your day brighter. Don't focus on the negative energy given off by some.

_____

_____

_____

_____

How I Matter

Our purpose here is to enrich the lives of those we care about. What did you do or could have
done to be a blessing for others today?

_____

_____

_____

_____

DATE: _____

Counting your Blessings

Each day offers many blessings. We can easily miss them in our daily toils.
Appreciate them here, no matter how small they may seem.

_____
_____
_____
_____

People that Matter

The people in our life plays a tremendous role in our personal happiness. Recognize them here and
how they made your day brighter. Don't focus on the negative energy given off by some.

_____
_____
_____
_____

How I Matter

Our purpose here is to enrich the lives of those we care about. What did you do or could have
done to be a blessing for others today?

_____
_____
_____
_____

DATE: _____

Counting your Blessings

Each day offers many blessings. We can easily miss them in our daily toils.
Appreciate them here, no matter how small they may seem.

_____

_____

_____

_____

People that Matter

The people in our life plays a tremendous role in our personal happiness. Recognize them here and
how they made your day brighter. Don't focus on the negative energy given off by some.

_____

_____

_____

_____

How I Matter

Our purpose here is to enrich the lives of those we care about. What did you do or could have
done to be a blessing for others today?

_____

_____

_____

_____

DATE: _____

Counting your Blessings

Each day offers many blessings. We can easily miss them in our daily toils.
Appreciate them here, no matter how small they may seem.

_____

_____

_____

People that Matter

The people in our life plays a tremendous role in our personal happiness. Recognize them here and
how they made your day brighter. Don't focus on the negative energy given off by some.

_____

_____

_____

How I Matter

Our purpose here is to enrich the lives of those we care about. What did you do or could have
done to be a blessing for others today?

_____

_____

_____

DATE: _____

Counting your Blessings

Each day offers many blessings. We can easily miss them in our daily toils.
Appreciate them here, no matter how small they may seem.

_____

_____

_____

People that Matter

The people in our life plays a tremendous role in our personal happiness. Recognize them here and
how they made your day brighter. Don't focus on the negative energy given off by some.

_____

_____

_____

How I Matter

Our purpose here is to enrich the lives of those we care about. What did you do or could have
done to be a blessing for others today?

_____

_____

_____

_____

DATE: _____

Counting your Blessings

Each day offers many blessings. We can easily miss them in our daily toils.
Appreciate them here, no matter how small they may seem.

_____
_____
_____

People that Matter

The people in our life plays a tremendous role in our personal happiness. Recognize them here and
how they made your day brighter. Don't focus on the negative energy given off by some.

_____
_____
_____

How I Matter

Our purpose here is to enrich the lives of those we care about. What did you do or could have
done to be a blessing for others today?

_____
_____
_____

DATE: _____

Counting your Blessings

Each day offers many blessings. We can easily miss them in our daily toils.
Appreciate them here, no matter how small they may seem.

_____

_____

_____

_____

People that Matter

The people in our life plays a tremendous role in our personal happiness. Recognize them here and
how they made your day brighter. Don't focus on the negative energy given off by some.

_____

_____

_____

_____

How I Matter

Our purpose here is to enrich the lives of those we care about. What did you do or could have
done to be a blessing for others today?

_____

_____

_____

_____

DATE: _____

Counting your Blessings

Each day offers many blessings. We can easily miss them in our daily toils.
Appreciate them here, no matter how small they may seem.

_____

_____

_____

People that Matter

The people in our life plays a tremendous role in our personal happiness. Recognize them here and
how they made your day brighter. Don't focus on the negative energy given off by some.

_____

_____

_____

How I Matter

Our purpose here is to enrich the lives of those we care about. What did you do or could have
done to be a blessing for others today?

_____

_____

_____

DATE: _____

Counting your Blessings

Each day offers many blessings. We can easily miss them in our daily toils.
Appreciate them here, no matter how small they may seem.

_____

_____

_____

People that Matter

The people in our life plays a tremendous role in our personal happiness. Recognize them here and
how they made your day brighter. Don't focus on the negative energy given off by some.

_____

_____

_____

How I Matter

Our purpose here is to enrich the lives of those we care about. What did you do or could have
done to be a blessing for others today?

_____

_____

_____

DATE: _____

Counting your Blessings

Each day offers many blessings. We can easily miss them in our daily toils.
Appreciate them here, no matter how small they may seem.

_____

_____

_____

People that Matter

The people in our life plays a tremendous role in our personal happiness. Recognize them here and
how they made your day brighter. Don't focus on the negative energy given off by some.

_____

_____

_____

How I Matter

Our purpose here is to enrich the lives of those we care about. What did you do or could have
done to be a blessing for others today?

_____

_____

_____

DATE: _____

Counting your Blessings

Each day offers many blessings. We can easily miss them in our daily toils.
Appreciate them here, no matter how small they may seem.

_____

_____

_____

People that Matter

The people in our life plays a tremendous role in our personal happiness. Recognize them here and
how they made your day brighter. Don't focus on the negative energy given off by some.

_____

_____

_____

How I Matter

Our purpose here is to enrich the lives of those we care about. What did you do or could have
done to be a blessing for others today?

_____

_____

_____

DATE: _____

Counting your Blessings

Each day offers many blessings. We can easily miss them in our daily toils.
Appreciate them here, no matter how small they may seem.

_____

_____

_____

People that Matter

The people in our life plays a tremendous role in our personal happiness. Recognize them here and
how they made your day brighter. Don't focus on the negative energy given off by some.

_____

_____

_____

How I Matter

Our purpose here is to enrich the lives of those we care about. What did you do or could have
done to be a blessing for others today?

_____

_____

_____

DATE: _____

Counting your Blessings

Each day offers many blessings. We can easily miss them in our daily toils.
Appreciate them here, no matter how small they may seem.

_____

_____

_____

People that Matter

The people in our life plays a tremendous role in our personal happiness. Recognize them here and
how they made your day brighter. Don't focus on the negative energy given off by some.

_____

_____

_____

How I Matter

Our purpose here is to enrich the lives of those we care about. What did you do or could have
done to be a blessing for others today?

_____

_____

_____

DATE: _____

Counting your Blessings

Each day offers many blessings. We can easily miss them in our daily toils.
Appreciate them here, no matter how small they may seem.

_____
_____
_____

People that Matter

The people in our life plays a tremendous role in our personal happiness. Recognize them here and
how they made your day brighter. Don't focus on the negative energy given off by some.

_____
_____
_____

How I Matter

Our purpose here is to enrich the lives of those we care about. What did you do or could have
done to be a blessing for others today?

_____
_____
_____

DATE: _____

Counting your Blessings

Each day offers many blessings. We can easily miss them in our daily toils.
Appreciate them here, no matter how small they may seem.

_____

_____

_____

People that Matter

The people in our life plays a tremendous role in our personal happiness. Recognize them here and
how they made your day brighter. Don't focus on the negative energy given off by some.

_____

_____

_____

How I Matter

Our purpose here is to enrich the lives of those we care about. What did you do or could have
done to be a blessing for others today?

_____

_____

_____

_____

DATE: _____

Counting your Blessings

Each day offers many blessings. We can easily miss them in our daily toils.
Appreciate them here, no matter how small they may seem.

_____

_____

_____

People that Matter

The people in our life plays a tremendous role in our personal happiness. Recognize them here and
how they made your day brighter. Don't focus on the negative energy given off by some.

_____

_____

_____

How I Matter

Our purpose here is to enrich the lives of those we care about. What did you do or could have
done to be a blessing for others today?

_____

_____

_____

DATE: _____

Counting your Blessings

Each day offers many blessings. We can easily miss them in our daily toils.
Appreciate them here, no matter how small they may seem.

_____

_____

_____

People that Matter

The people in our life plays a tremendous role in our personal happiness. Recognize them here and
how they made your day brighter. Don't focus on the negative energy given off by some.

_____

_____

_____

How I Matter

Our purpose here is to enrich the lives of those we care about. What did you do or could have
done to be a blessing for others today?

_____

_____

_____

DATE: _____

Counting your Blessings

Each day offers many blessings. We can easily miss them in our daily toils.
Appreciate them here, no matter how small they may seem.

_____

_____

_____

People that Matter

The people in our life plays a tremendous role in our personal happiness. Recognize them here and
how they made your day brighter. Don't focus on the negative energy given off by some.

_____

_____

_____

How I Matter

Our purpose here is to enrich the lives of those we care about. What did you do or could have
done to be a blessing for others today?

_____

_____

_____

DATE: _____

Counting your Blessings

Each day offers many blessings. We can easily miss them in our daily toils.
Appreciate them here, no matter how small they may seem.

_____

_____

_____

People that Matter

The people in our life plays a tremendous role in our personal happiness. Recognize them here and
how they made your day brighter. Don't focus on the negative energy given off by some.

_____

_____

_____

How I Matter

Our purpose here is to enrich the lives of those we care about. What did you do or could have
done to be a blessing for others today?

_____

_____

_____

Made in the USA
Monee, IL
19 May 2022

96687515R10068